Author: Brigitte Kohrs

My Biography

All data are from 1973

and correspond to the truth!

A Mother's Heart Never Forgets - Forced Adoption in the BRD
& The Search Continues!

Author: Brigitte Kohrs

Impressum

Bibliografische Information der Deutschen Nationalbibliothek:
Die Deutsche Nationalbibliothek verzeichnet diese Publikation
in der Deutschen Nationalbibliografie; detaillierte
bibliografische Daten sind im Internet über http://dnb.dnb.de
abrufbar.

© 2023 Brigitte Kohrs

Lektorat: Robert Andre`Kohrs
Korrektorat: Brigitte Kohrs

Herstellung und Verlag: BoD – Books on Demand,
Norderstedt

ISBN: 9783757878412

Table of Contents

Foreword

Dear Reader
A mother's heart never forgets Forced adoption in the FRG &
The search goes on!
And my search continued until 2019.
9 more years of hope and anxiety to finally have certainty, where my daughter lived and whether she is well today, was the big question, which also surely asked each of my loyal readers?!
I have promised you all, in my first book, the search for my daughter continues until I have certainty and now be curious about whether I have made it. Me against the authorities and Jugendämter, which as always have put obstacles in my way, with strong will to achieve my goal?!
They have tormented me, lied to me and wanted to dissuade me from my search with all means at his disposal, but a mother's heart never forgets!
The search goes on! My goal is to give my son the opportunity to meet his biological sister, whom he had to do without for decades! Whether I have made it, stands here in my biography!

For decades I have been looking for my daughter, who was born on 16.09.1973, in Berlin - Neukölln together with her identical twin sister, who unfortunately died after her birth. I had to endure the pain of losing my little daughter because she died after birth and I had to endure the pain of having my second daughter torn away from me in a brutal way planned by the Jugendamt immediately after delivery! What kind of pain and humiliation can a person endure at the hands of these people? A lot, if you don't lose sight of your goal and love your child with all your heart. Well for this reason I did not give up, until today, in July 2019. But I was not used to it any other way! For decades, the authorities and youth welfare offices literally went sledding with me and my feelings. Always, the conversations I tried to have with them were accompanied by an icy coldness. Feelings, or being a mother, did not play a role in their adoption jungle, only the adoption laws counted and therefore the fear of showing some humanity ruled over them all. But I know all their tricks and excuses! They want to unsettle me and scatter wrong directions! It is like in a nightmare that does not want to end. You don't get me down, because you've been trying to do that for decades, but I keep coming back until you tell me where my daughter is! This will never be and has never been a walk in the park because there are too many working against me and my good intentions to find my child. What have I done that you treat me so unworthily?

I was only 15 years old and I was completely alienated! I gave birth to her and I am her mother and she has my roots. I will continue to search for her and I will find her because fate will not allow what you have been doing to me for decades with your cover-ups and lies! I will find my daughter! The search goes on and you will not prevent it, not even with your adoption laws! With your fear to help parents of origin, nor to support them in a positive direction. There are many promises. But what remains are speech bubbles and only empty words! I call you and you let your colleagues slander you and they support you! The youth welfare office, your friend and helper? Unfortunately not for parents of origin, rather for adoptive parents! We, the parents of origin are only the incubators for your adoptive parents and afterwards we are disposed of like garbage. In incognito adoptions, the true identity of the child is erased! What is the matter with you? You create an illusion - identity, without consideration, on the child, or its origin family and do also still so hypocritical, as if the true family of the adoptive child does not exist any more, or still much worse, ignores the origin roots of the adopted ones! I would be pleased for my person and also other origin parents, if you reconsider your so perfect adoption laws for the adoption parents and for the well-being of the children, which should stand with all questions and answers, in the first place, also for the so numerous origin parents, in order to decide with honesty, for the well-being of the child.

Is it right to take away the children's roots of origin and let them grow up with a life lie? This is not for the good of a child, but damages his/her soul! It is said that the invisible umbilical cord between mother and child will always be a connection, for a lifetime! Also no adoption laws, or your Ausforschungsverbot §1758 change it. Now where I sit here at my PC and write the continuation of my decade-long search for my daughter, I become conscious, what I had to go through again for 9 years with these authorities humanly, in order to reach my goal! Once/twice hell and back! It is 2019 and nothing has changed for me since 1973. I wished it so much - to get help and support about the youth welfare office, but no where, because to the good end I stand again mother souls alone there, with scanty, or no information, what really happened in 1973 with my daughter. Okay, I have tried to get help and support from you, now the search continues as before alone with my numerous searches. But how, is here the question, because easier it would have been with the official help for me and my daughter. But why simply, if the youth welfare department can make the life even more difficult for me, because I am only her bodily mother! I take my folders, where I have collected all my research over decades, so as not to take double steps.

Because this search robs me of strength on some days! How often did I want to give up?! I had to take longer search breaks. These breaks I needed urgently, otherwise I could not have continued my decades-long search! Now my readers might ask themselves? What drove this woman to search for her daughter for decades? Very simple answer - The love for my children, never let me give up searching for my beloved daughter. I have always felt that there is still someone of us out there, who may feel something warm in his heart, as I do! The way was long and hard that I had behind me and it should become even harder. Thanks to the people who first gave me hints and took them away again the other day. A roller coaster of feelings in which I was pushed again and again by strange people, from whom I hoped for help and support, in my complicated search, in the cold! How often I wanted to end this search, because it tormented me so and I had the feeling, it goes nothing more, I got up again the next day and wanted to fight on to find it! Whenever I gave up and didn't want to go on because I was so disappointed in everyone, it was as if a door opened and a light shone through it, giving me the strength not to give up and to keep searching for my daughter. When I started searching for my daughter decades ago.

I was aware that I would not get much support in my search.
 my search. But that I would get almost no help and support,
I was at no time so much aware, as where I was in the middle
of my search actions. It was an up and down of my emotional
world! Enough whining, the search continues! But how, that
was my question?! I searched for decades my daughter and
had accordingly by my searches, some information gathered,
but no real proof. I got from my mother the written statement,
from whom my daughter from the children's hospital - 4 days
after the birth was fetched and that she was taken with the
family of the bodily father to West Germany to the relatives.
Then I knew from stories that a kinship from West Germany,
at the Youth Welfare Office in the place of residence, have
applied as an adoptive family! The problem is that these
statements were credible, but if you have no written
documents about it, it is for the outside world, only allegations
and I needed proof! How should I continue the search for my
daughter and where would I get support?! I must honestly say,
I had a big question mark, hovering over my head! But come
time, come advice! I fetched the greatest treasure

from my file folder, my mother's passport, without it I could never have started my search.

 I was lied to and cheated out of my daughter by everyone at the women's clinic in Neukölln in 1973. bad enough that my twin girl died after birth, but to then let me live with the thought that both children are dead is the greatest sin that has been committed by people against me, really evil! There is no excuse, or excuses for that, for the sake of the child! Life lies for the sake of my daughter?! I didn't want my daughter to live with a life lie all her life and that's why I had to keep looking for my daughter. I do not give up and is the further way just as stony, or stonier I fight for my daughter no matter how old she is today, because she is and remains my child! No adoptive parents, or adoption laws will change that. My old mother's passport from 1973 was the door to my daughter. Through this document, I was finally able to prove that my daughter was alive! The heart sound that was entered into my maternal passport on 09/18/1973 was the proof! I believe in the fate and it did not want to separate my daughter and her family finally! My mother's passport, which actually should disappear in the shredder of the hospital is for me the proof that I should never give up my daughter! And fortunately I never did, because the love for my child was always bigger and stronger than the obstacles I was confronted with in my search. True love, can move mountains!

 Not only I as a mother, my dear son and my dear family has been cheated of the sister and our family member with our roots quite badly. My son even if he always acts so cool also suffers from it and misses his biological sister! Also my son was always a big drive my daughter and his sister further to search. I love my children with all my heart and would never have given my little daughter to other people, but at 15 I had no say! But even at 15 I tried to find my daughter in the hospital! I looked at me to the X - times my mother passport of 1973 and saw completely down under the date 18.09.1973 a measurement, which was written down from a number and % in my mother passport, but of whom and what stood there for a name, as signature. I puzzled back and forth and when I was sure, I researched in the media. I found a gynecologist there who could match this name from my maternity record and immediately called his office in Berlin Steglitz. I briefly described my concern and got an appointment with him at the practice on the same day. With my heart pounding and my maternity passport in my pocket, I took the subway from Berlin Rudow to Steglitz! I was so excited and wondered the whole time of the subway ride, whether he will be my savior, to to find my daughter! When I arrived at the gynecologist's office with a beating heart together with a good friend who was to be my witness during the conversation with the gynecologist.

 When I arrived at the gynecologist's office with a beating heart, together with a good friend who was to be my witness during the conversation with the gynecologist, it did not take very long and the gynecologist, who was a stranger to me, called me into his office. With trembling hands and tears in my eyes, I handed him my great treasure, my maternity passport, and told him my cruel story about it. He looked at me stunned and also he did not understand the world in this moment of my stories. He looked very attentively at my maternity record of 1973 and what he noticed immediately that my complete pregnancy of the twins has been neatly separated out. He noticed it because my maternity record was untypically thin! Then the gynecologist looked carefully at the date, the 18.09.1973 and the measured value in % numbers and then came for me the redeeming sentence. This is a heart sound measurement of a newborn, as far as I know, but I am not a pediatrician. It was a hope for me that my daughter was alive! His eyes moved further down and now he examined very carefully, the signature of the doctor under the heart tone measurement, from 18.09.1973. He was very pleased to be able to tell me that he even knows this pediatrician from the children's clinic in Neukölln personally and so he was now also sure that it was a heart tone measurement from my baby. That special moment, when a doctor confirmed that my daughter was alive, was for me

 like Christmas Pentecost and Easter in one day! Now I was crying with happiness! The very friendly and helpful gynecologist gave me the name and address of the pediatrician and I drove home overjoyed with this great news! I first had to recover from all the excitement and except for my good friend, I didn't tell anyone about it for fear that someone might take it from me. So I also guarded my maternity passport, because it was the door to my missing daughter. The next day I looked for the pediatrician's phone number in the phone book and had my friend call there because I was so afraid of being disappointed again. But I stood very close to the phone and listened in on the conversation, which sounded positive. I couldn't stand to hear all about my daughter! My friend handed me the phone. This pediatrician, after so many years that had passed, could remember exactly 9/16/1973 and my twin birth and that I was only 15 years old at the time of the birth. He immediately enlightened me that he had performed a heart tone measurement on my daughter and was surprised that my maternity record showed birth weights that were much too low. He then entered my daughter's heart sound measurement from 18.09.1973 and immediately noted the too low birth weight.

Birth weights changed and an old German ZW. written in front of it,

which was the truth. One daughter has 2450g and the surviving daughter weighed 2500g at birth. The pediatrician also confirmed that my one twin daughter unfortunately did not survive! Now I had the certainty that one daughter unfortunately died after birth and my other daughter survived. I had one laughing eye and one crying eye when I heard about it from the pediatrician from the pediatric clinic in Berlin Neukölln. I was so grateful to fate that I had my maternity passport from 1973 and found the pediatrician who knew my case exactly through the friendly and helpful gynecologist from Berlin Steglitz. I thanked very much the pediatrician of my daughter from 1973, who also gave me the important hint that my daughter was picked up by the family of the biological father after 4 days stay in the pediatric clinic and that they wanted to go to West Germany with my baby immediately, because they were already waiting there! I felt, like the happiest woman and mother on the whole earth, because I had come in my years of search, finally a large piece further and could by the pediatrician finally clear up and get confirmed, which survived a girl of my twin birth on 16.09.1973. I could now rearrange everything and knew that I had to look for a daughter and all uncertainties, whether my other daughter also survived, were proven by the

 facts of the pediatrician about my twin birth on 16.09.1973 proved. For me it was certain that my search for my daughter continues! Since I always am and also was a safety-conscious person and wanted to secure myself doubly, I contacted the heart center in Berlin and checked again whether it is also 100% a heart sound measurement? The doctor from the pediatric cardiology confirmed to me that it is a heart sound measurement of my daughter and also that she lives with this heart sound value! The cardiologist confirmed this to me again in writing, which my daughter's pediatrician had also confirmed to me verbally. Now I have the proof that my daughter survived, but this will not be enough to convince the authorities! I felt where my daughter grew up! This was just the tip of the iceberg and I knew that I was far from the end of my search and once again I was to be proven right! The stones that still lay before me, I could not estimate in this moment of being happy, yet. I received a decisive hint from my daughter's pediatrician that my daughter had survived and that was enough motivation not to end the search, but to continue looking for my daughter! I was so excited and satisfied that my years of searching have now borne fruit.

has. Also because the love for my child motivated me and gave me the strength not to give up.

 I had to think very carefully about my next steps, because as a mother of origin I could not legally expect any information from the authorities. I also always had great hope that my daughter would look for me. She would get information about her origin if she wanted to meet us. Then this thought came to me?! What if she doesn't know at all that she was adopted?! Then she grew up in an ideal world, with a life lie. How cruel! I didn't want to think about it and had hope that her adoptive parents didn't hide the truth from her. I called a good acquaintance and asked for advice, because she was a person who knew a lot about adoption! I had always told her only rudiments of my cruel story, but this time I took it upon myself to tell my story from the beginning, hoping she could give me advice and support, and I was lucky! It was a good day, because she had time for me and so I told her what had happened to me on 16.09.1973 in the women's clinic with my twins. That I found the pediatrician, I still kept like a secret! She listened to me attentively and that did me unspeakably good! My acquaintance, who is also active in the social area, was shocked, over my cruel experiences, from the birth to the child removal! She was speechless for minutes and it did me unspeakably good to feel this understanding and their consternation about my

 cruel experiences! Finally a person on my stony paths, who no longer understands the world and she said, in a low voice - Oh God, how could they do such a thing to you! There would have been probably also 1973 other ways, than to proceed so radically, soon already criminally. I noticed her shock at this for a long time and it was a long time before she could speak normally. She knew exactly that nobody can ignore these firmly established adoption laws and with an incognito adoption, which was usual with infants 1973, still less, to no information could be found. But she was ready to support me, in a very legal way. I ended the conversation, because these conversations stirred me up very much and each time, I experienced the past anew! The past sounds so past, but how should one's own child belong to the past! There are no recipes and no good advice! Only understanding and support can help! I had enough good advice - support rather less. After a few days my phone rang and my friend was on the phone. I was so happy that she called me and also very curious if she could help me. She had good news! She had researched and there it occurred to her that in a portal on the Internet there is a call from adopted twins who were born in 1973 in Berlin and search for their family of origin. So much, as I was happy about this positive news, I had in my

 back of my mind that my one daughter of my twins, died after birth, according to the pediatrician of the children's hospital with whom I had contact before my acquaintance! Then the thought of distrust crept in again and I thought?! I was only lied to and deceived by the women's clinic and the authorities. Is the story true that a daughter died after birth?! There it was again, the great insecurity in me! I should have believed the pediatrician! Then I would have saved myself a lot of chaos. But somehow it was fate that I met these twins, who were born in Berlin in 1973 and were also adopted to West Germany, as it will turn out! My acquaintance gave me the portal where this very recent call was posted and I wrote an email to one of these seeking twins. I didn't have to wait long and the first email came from the searcher for her family of origin. It was immediately a lively and friendly exchange of our 1973 information. We got along very well and it was a good fit. My hope that both children were still alive was high at that time! But as they say, hope dies in the end. I must honestly say that I enjoyed this time of lively exchange by E - mail. Always connected with the great hope to have found my children.

In the meantime, I no longer wanted to think about what the pediatrician told me during our last conversation.

 our last conversation, that only one daughter survived. I always had this feeling that they are not 100% my twins, but there was also the feeling that I should not end the e-mail contact. After three months of lively e-mail contact, I noticed that I and the seeker of their family of origin, never talked about it, in the meantime we also talked on the phone, when the twins were born in 1973 in Berlin and in which hospital?! We were all so happy to have found each other that we sweep the facts under the table, but we couldn't! We were all looking for a loved one. I my daughter and the twins from Berlin, their mother and family of origin. 3 months had passed after the first contact and we talked on the phone more often! I had to do it! To ask the questions, of all questions, to clarify the facts. I felt that this time was getting closer and closer, but what was still missing to have the courage to ask these questions for clarification. I wanted to wait a little longer and that was my right decision, as it would turn out later on my further ways. It was July 2015 and a sunny day when I once again spoke with the seeker on the phone. It was a lively exchange of information until I paid attention. She told me that she, in West Germany with her twin sister in a

Oberschule went, where she completed her ABI. One class and one floor above them in this

 Oberschule, she suddenly mentioned the name of a young woman who was also born in 1973 and who was very well known to her. I listened attentively to her stories and thought, that's not possible! I thought, this is not true now, because this young woman was also known to me, because she has crossed my ways for decades in stories from the family. What does this mean, I asked myself? Does my assumption over decades become now by this conversation the truth? I asked probably 5 more times whether she knows exactly that this young woman was born in 1973 and whether the name is correct. She said again and again that she is very sure and her statements correspond to the truth. Now I knew what fate wanted to tell me and why I maintained contact with the twins for 3 months. It was no coincidence that I had to learn all this. How the life plays in such a way! We ended this conversation in a friendly way and I thanked him very much for this information. Now I also had the feeling to clarify the rest of uncertainties with the seeker and I did that a week later. We had gotten along so well that she thought I was her mother and here and there, I thought so too. But the fate brought us together for a special reason, to confirm the information of the pediatrician that my one daughter survives has. In a longer conversation, we then clarified the facts and unfortunately had to find out that, although

 some things agreed, but they were not born in September 1973 and also not in the women's clinic in which I gave birth. A few weeks later I received the info that these twins had received a call from the youth welfare office that their family of origin had been found! I was so happy for them and wished them all the best. I was very happy that I was allowed to meet the two of them and learn such interesting news from them, which should really bring me further in the search for my beloved daughter - destiny! Unfortunately, contact with the twins broke off immediately after that! I think that they were so happy to have found their family of origin, that the contact with me, should remain a good memory on both sides. My search went on with fresh courage in the luggage, because who rests, that rusts! My next thought was, how should I arrange my search in the near future and whom should I contact to get support?! This will not be easy, the thoughts raced through my head. I started again to research on the Internet! Predominantly one finds there adopted ones, which look for their families of origin and in addition also assistance of the offices and authorities get, marvelously! Unfortunately, the page of the parents of origin, on the other hand, looks rather black and the offers of help are very thin, until not present. Now I saw already again before my mental eye, the stones, which were put to me

 already for decades in the way were put, because of the anchored adoption laws! Yes, the dear adoption laws, which made life difficult for me as an origin mother to find my child. But not to give up and complain, but to stand up and fight on, that was my guiding principle! How else could I have searched for my daughter for decades?! Then the idea was there how I will continue my search. I contacted the family court! It was like torture, because every day I waited for a call, or mail from the family court from West Germany, but nothing happened. I had trouble sleeping because I was so afraid that no one would get in touch with me from there and that I would get nowhere with my search, as I had done so many times over the years. It was a decades-long puzzle, searching for my child, whom I missed so much. I have thought of my little daughter every day since her birth on Sept. 16, 1973, and how wonderfully she cried immediately after her birth. It was like a cry of protest because they mercilessly, immediately, when I perceived her briefly, forcibly stunned me with the ether mask. I can still see this giant hand on my small narrow face, with the ether mask and another hand turned the bottle in which was the anesthetic, higher and higher, until I had nothing noticed more and was completely stunned! Is that humane and permissible at all? That is in the

 Basic Law - The dignity of man is inviolable? And what was with my dignity, or the dignity of my little daughter? Every newborn baby needs its mother and not strangers! I carried my children in my belly for 9 months and loved them more than anything! I didn't smoke, no alcohol, ate healthy food. I did everything for my twins to be born healthy and the reward for me was a bucket of bad luck, from the authorities. What evil did I do, or what did my girl do that she was not allowed to stay with her mother? 15 years and too young is no excuse for what has been done to me, my son and my daughter for a lifetime! After my son, her biological brother was never asked! He suffers and he misses his sister, but who cares, it's not about his own life, it's just a Jugendamt file with a number! I think so because if you knock on doors for years that remain closed, then the past runs like a movie. No human being on this earth forgets such negative experiences! She is my child! She has my roots and the roots of her family of origin. Adoption laws don't change anything and mother feelings can't disappear in youth welfare office files, because a mother heart never forgets! After 14 days of endless waiting for the longed-for answer from the family court in West Germany,

I picked up the phone and called the employee in charge at the family court. She was in a hurry, at least that's what she said. When she could classify who I am and what I want from her, she hurriedly choked me off with the words! I'll check on her process. Then she checked again whether I had sent my request in writing to the family court. When that was so far to her satisfaction, she said in an unfriendly voice, "I can't give you any information on the phone now. You will receive a written decision from the specialist department in the next few days. I wanted to thank her, but she quickly hung up after this sentence. After all, I thought, urgent information is better than no information. Now I was curious to see what the family court would send me in writing. 3 days later came the written decision from the court! I was very excited when I finally held the long-awaited letter in my hand. I did not dare to open it and kept holding it in my hand. Then the thoughts raced through my head, what does it say? After much deliberation and emotional chaos between fear and joy, I opened the official letter. How many of these so-called official letters have I received in the last years of my search? There was mostly the same written Due to the Personal Data Protection Act, we are not allowed to give them information about people, or adoptions, unless there is a public interest. They would then have to make that credible in their application.

 These were constantly the same stones blocking my way to look for my daughter. But I am a mother who loves her child and a lioness who defends her family. I don't give up and you don't scare me with your rules and adoption laws, because I am the woman who gave birth to her, her mother! Now I held in my hands the letter I had been waiting for weeks. At first I skimmed the sentences for fear it could be another friendly rejection on my request. Are there still people who have a heart and feelings for a desperate mother who is looking for her child? There was an approval procedure at our family court in 1974 in the name??? I could not believe my eyes and there it was, the name of my little daughter! I cried - screamed with joy and whirled around my living room with the letter in my hand! This clue was worth gold for me! Because now I knew where my way of the search will lead me and from assumptions, became certainty. A great success! But also on this success, I could not rest, because the search had to go further. What should be my next step? I had to think carefully so as not to make any mistakes, because I am a mother of origin, and as we all know, the doors of the office remain firmly closed. Fortunately, the very strict adoption laws of 1973, were changed for the better by 2019.

and if one meets friendly youth welfare office coworkers with a heart for parents of origin, then also here one endeavors to support the family of origin. As is well known, there are certainly numerous individual cases where the mothers, like me in 1973, were only minors at the birth of their child and were just as externally determined as I was. They certainly wanted to keep their child themselves, I am convinced of that. I wanted to go legal ways to find my daughter and also kept to respecting the adoption laws. Even if it was sometimes difficult for me and I saw myself as a victim. It always built me up when I received conditional support and guidance from some authorities even as an origin mother. My puzzle became more and more each time and there was always a piece added, even if it was very exhausting! I had set myself a goal, to find my daughter! I needed to know if my daughter was okay and if she was told she was adopted! I was tormented by the thought that my child had not been informed that her mother existed. Now I finally felt like I was getting somewhere with finding my daughter! I finally found out important facts that will surely take me further than before! I felt that my search was finally making progress and I did not stop in one place and all doors remained closed and little changed in the course of my years.

Search for my daughter changed. What did I have left of her birth? An old maternity passport from 1973, with little information about the birth and zero information about my entire preventive examinations of the pregnancy from 1973! Exactly these pages, were removed from my maternity passport, by whoever? Nevertheless, my old maternity passport was really a great help! First, the entry in my mother's passport from the pediatrician who had performed a heart tone measurement on my daughter at Children's Hospital in 1973. This enabled me to do further research. Then came the notice from the family court and the meeting with the twins who were looking for their family of origin. All of them gave me valuable hints, for which I am so very grateful! These so valuable hints brought me a bit closer to my daughter each time. Resting was not, because the search for my daughter had to go on, because I wanted it to! I got a lot of hints during my decade-long search for my child. However, I could not apply every piece of advice, no matter how well-intentioned, to my further search, because I had to and also wanted to follow the adoption laws. There is no sense in getting mail from a lawyer! Paragraph 1758 is used very gladly with the incognito - adoption! In other words zero chance to find his incognito adopted child, or abundant perseverance and willpower, but that is not quite enough, unfortunately! Research and hopes for support from people who have a

 heart for poor parents of origin! From my long search experiences for my incognito adopted beloved daughter, I can say to it that it is not easy to find these people, but also not impossible! I have experienced it in the same way during my search for my daughter. It is true that it is very difficult to tell the story of one's life to strangers about 100 times. But without these exact narrations one has no chance that someone becomes supportive active with this extremely heavy search! I have also experienced that people from authorities were very open and helpful to me, until the § 1758 appeared incognito - adoption and already the doors were closed and everything I was told and confirmed the day before, was a big mistake, or a misunderstanding from the day before! If this reaction came, then I thanked kindly and believed the statement of the employee from the previous day, because it matched my search 100%. It was very difficult to mislead me, because I had a lot of experiences with offices authorities and employees on my way of the search. It was basically always the same process and the same words when § 1758 came up. How should this go on and how should I ever find her! When should I find my incognito adopted daughter, if § 1758 makes my life so difficult?

made. I did not want to give up and my search had to continue even with § 1758. Thus I built § 1758 into my search, because I wanted to go the legal way. Desperately I was already sometimes, even if it looks at some places of my biography for the reader in such a way, as if I managed this with ease! No, it was not so! The decades-long search for my daughter, has cost me a lot of tears - despondency and despair! I also had to take longer breaks in my search because I was going in circles and not making any progress. Those were the worst times, when all doors remained closed and my facts were still too few to finally contact the responsible youth welfare office! So I had to fight on alone and that was very hard some days, not to give up but to keep looking. It was the love for my children that gave me the strength to this day and my husband, who has been behind me for 20 years and supports me morally! I am very grateful for that! An acquaintance of mine gave me the advice to contact a tracing service. Good idea I thought but first I wanted to contact the Jugendamt in West Germany! There was only one general adoption agency there, which I wanted to contact to explain my concern there! I had to research first because I wanted to contact the right office. Otherwise, I would have to tell my life story again X times and that wanted to

I could avoid. I had all the information together and now I called again with a beating heart the employee of the adoption agency in West Germany. Unfortunately, I reached on this day no one and so I decided to write an e-mail to the employee to describe my concern. Now came the big wait for the longed-for answer! I constantly looked in my e-mail box, but no message came from the employee of the adoption center from West Germany. My mood was in the cellar and I thought, always the same § 1758! The next day, finally, there was the message in my email inbox that I had to wait for 1 week after my call. I opened this e-mail excitedly and was immediately disappointed again! Short and sweet it was written there by the employee?! Call me on Thursday during my office hours! That did not sound very binding, but this reaction to my request, I was unfortunately used to. Thursday came and I was again excited and could hardly sleep at night. I called the employee the Thursday in her office hours. She tried to be friendly to me. However, I immediately noticed in the first few sentences we exchanged how cautious and meager her statements were about finding my daughter. Most of the time she listened to me and said nothing. That was 2015 and today it is 2019. By 2019, I had been in contact with this employee from the adoption center

from West Germany and when I think about it, in 4 years I have only gained fractions to my puzzle of the
 Search in addition won. But, the bird in the hand is better than the dove on the roof! 4 years were the so called learning phase for mothers of origin! But I was happy and grateful for this contact, which supported me over the years a huge piece in my search positive, even with § 1758. My advantage here was that I researched for decades on all forms of adoption and my experiences, the employee told and what I found out over the years. A semi-open, or open adoption, as was possible after 1973, would certainly have been less complicated in helping me find my daughter. Unfortunately, in 1973 incognito adoptions, especially with underage mothers, were still popular and then a new identity is written for the child, with the blessing of the guardianship court and the worst part of it all is that the family of origin loses all rights. The kinship relationship is erased. For me, this is a life lie for a child. The child does not even get a normal birth certificate, but a family record book entry with the adoptive parents! I do not find this legal, because the child belongs to the origin family and carries also these roots in itself! That is completely unworldly, these incognito - adoption laws! They make the life difficult for the family of origin and there are certainly also many individual cases,

as in my case, where contact with the family of origin could take place without endangering the welfare of the child!

 could take place! I can report today from my own experiences! If one investigated oneself and presents that to the youth welfare department, one is supported from there conditionally. I would like to say in addition that the coworkers of the central adoption switching offices, which support parents of origin, but unfortunately only conditionally! Conditionally will ask itself now the Leser/in? I would like to explain that here in my biography of the adoption paragraph jungle gladly. The coworkers of the central adoption places are willing to support the family of origin! They listen attentively to the circumstances of the adoption, must then think about it in a single case decision and weigh whether a child well-being endangerment can be excluded. This can, unfortunately, take years, because in my case, my Jugendamt files did not show up in the first years, or in other words, because § 1758 had prevented it. As we know, my daughter was adopted incognito against my will. § 1758 has burned itself over years into my head, because this paragraph tormented me infinitely and prevented me again and again to lead my search unharmed further! I was so annoyed by § 1758 that I wanted to end the search 1000 times, but there was this deep love for my daughter that I did not want to give up. That's why the search went on! I set myself goal for goal, in order to come forward in my search and that was for me puzzle work, for decades, unfortunately! I had very often telephone contact in these 4 years to the employee, the central adoption office from West Germany! Even if these conversations ran off predominantly in such a way that I only talked and told and she listened to me attentively, it did me unbelievably well! These cruelties, which were done to me in 1973 in the women's clinic in Berlin, I could process better through the conversations, with the employee, the Central Adoption Office from West Germany. These numerous conversations from 2015 - 2019 gave me strength and I no longer felt as lonely as before. And I felt that this help and support was honest, even if § 1758, the friendly employee repeatedly prevented me from giving more detailed information about the facts, but I could understand her! I felt that she not only listened to me, but that in the background, even without words, she understood my situation and wanted to support me from the bottom of my heart. That is why I contacted her again and again during these 4 years by e-mail, or by phone. The path of my search had become easier, because I no longer researched on my own, but contacted the Central Adoption Office in West Germany. I had also contacted the Central Adoption Office in Berlin years before.

and also had a personal appointment there. There, too, I explained the cruel circumstances for the incognito

 Adoption of my little daughter explained and also there the woman employee listened to me attentively. But also there § 1758 left my Jugendamt file closed! Therefore, I left the room of the Jugendamt employee very sad. She promised me to get in touch, which never happened and that's why I have completely lost confidence in the Jugendämter. Until 2015, these solo attempts to find my daughter were pre-programmed by this behavior towards me. I had not made the best experiences with the Youth Welfare Office of Berlin, because I owe it to this Youth Welfare Office that I have been looking for my daughter for decades, because they have decided to let an adoption - consent blank, which was not permissible, to sign under flimsy excuses. Is nevertheless really the very last with such methods children to the adoption freely to give! Since I was exactly informed about the fact that my daughter came to West Germany, the employee from Berlin gave me the advice to contact the central adoption offices in West Germany in the near future. After my experience with a staff member of the Central Adoption Office in Berlin, I no longer had the nerve to do so! I felt simply pushed off by the coworker. That she could keep the file closed in Berlin, I should move to West Germany. I was an uncomfortable

mother of origin, who actually, according to the adoption plan from the youth welfare office in Berlin, was never allowed to show up at their
 with them. Why? Because the plan was to shred my mother's passport still in the women's clinic on 17.09.1973, one day after the birth of my children in the consulting room of the gynecologist! But dear youth welfare department, I was faster, because I felt that a daughter survived and if you had not prevented me with these nurses, then my daughter would have grown up with her mother and her very dear family of origin and not with strange people! My child had to grow up with a life lie! No one can make it up to her! My beloved daughter and I her mother have become victims of your official mills incl. § 1758. You will never be able to understand how we all suffer and how it hurts for a lifetime that an intact family was torn apart so badly. You have taken away the daughter from the mother and the sister from the biological brother. The nephew, the aunt! The grandma, the granddaughter and the aunt the niece. Also all the others from our family, an important family member! My daughter has two families due to her involuntary and very controversial incognito adoption. An adoption family and an origin family! No one wants to take anything away from us, we just wish to be a part of her life as a family of origin with her roots! Who gives you all the right to do this,

To ban us from her life?! We are her family too and she has every right in the world. To know her family of origin and her roots. You are not God, or our destiny! After these experiences, with the Central Adoption Office in Berlin it took until 2015 until I decided to contact the Central Adoption Office in West Germany and there I found more understanding for what had been done to me and my little daughter by the Youth Welfare Office in Berlin. After a short period of intensive discussions with the employee, I knew that I would maintain this contact. At no time did she make promises to me that she could not keep and I could always rely on her word over the years. It was slow going, but it was going! This reliability of the youth welfare office employee counted for me and I felt better. I felt with the whole situation, no longer lonely and offers of help to find my child. She showed me that a Jugendamt employee, if he/she works with a lot of understanding and empathy and deals honestly with his/her counterpart, achieves more than our famous § 1758. Humanity is important in such cases and no § 1758 law teachings. It concerns here with each individual adoption case humans and sensitive feelings to their children. Dear Jugendamt employees! A little more feeling and understanding for the desperate parents of origin who contact you and ask for support! Support should not only be a nice word, but also please be put into action.

 be put into action. There stand very desperate people, like me, who just want to build a contact with their incognito adopted child, because everyone loves his child! No matter what circumstances led to adoption. A mother's heart never forgets! Despite the fact that I had a really good contact with the Central Adoption Office in West Germany, I did not want to stand still in the search for my daughter and even with the support of the staff, I wanted to keep searching. My confidence was not set very high and I only believed what I got confirmed in writing, which happened rather seldom, or what I experienced personally in the numerous telephone calls with offices and authorities. This was my security to control my search. I contacted some offices and authorities in writing during the years of my search. Most of the answers were negative and related to the Personal Status Law, which of course is related to our beloved? § 1758 related! I hate this paragraph, which always gets in my way in my search and overturns everything I want to find with its stubbornness. But I do not give up! Here and there a compassionate door opened and then I also got once a positive message, which should lead me further in my search. One piece of the puzzle comes to the other and that made me infinitely happy! This information was helpful, but were still far from sufficient to prove where my daughter grew up. I knew it, but I had to prove it to the Jugendamt, so they would have to drop their masks to finally support me in the right direction for me. They knew it, but I as the mother of origin had to prove that I had found out where my daughter had arrived after her birth and I had known that for years! My mother had confirmed in writing when and where my daughter had arrived after her birth and I sent this letter to the Jugendamt staff! They didn't really like this statement, but what could they do about it? My mother was my key witness. I was so grateful to my mother, because she was the only one who told me the whole truth decades later, but better late than never, and who was infinitely sorry that she had to lie to me in the name of the Youth Welfare Office of Berlin, because she was put under pressure by the Youth Welfare Office of Berlin. If my parents should not agree to an adoption, to accommodate me in a home and then still with an announcement because of supervision obligation injury, because I became pregnant with 15 years. What was my mother supposed to do? What would other mothers have done? Still, my mother kept saying that it wouldn't be a problem because she could work half days and that I would take care of my child. But that was already a decided thing! We got no chance, nevertheless we were an intact family and my daughter would have had it well they gave us no chance! My newborn baby was torn from me mercilessly immediately after birth and came to the children's ward in the children's hospital of the women's clinic in Berlin, for 4 days! After 4 days - the statement of the pediatrician, who cared for my daughter for 4 days and also performed her heart tone measurement, my little girl was taken away from the family?! This was also confirmed to me by my mother. My newborn daughter was taken away to West Germany, that's how I see it! Excuse me! Of course with all good wishes and the holy blessing from the youth welfare office in Berlin - Neukölln! Not to forget that my mother's passport should disappear. According to the motto out of sight, out of mind, but not with me! There the calculation was probably made without the mother of origin. I have from the day on their birth, on 16.09.1973 my small girl never forgotten and them searched. You have taken two children from me! One daughter has died and the other surviving daughter you have taken from me in addition? How do you all feel about it? Simply given up for incognito adoption, against my will. So I lost both my girls on the same day. The difference is?! One was decided by fate and the other happened by human hand, because my second daughter is alive! Even if in the meantime in my anger and hurt seemed to sink, the search for my child should not come to a standstill.

 When a person is desperate, he/she tries to clutch at any straw and gladly accepts any outside advice. I contacted a detective agency that also searched for missing adoptees at home and abroad. I described my concern and also honestly what had been done to me in 1973. Everyone was sorry, but there, too, Section 1758 prevented them from starting the search. Unfortunately, I then got to a detective agency, for which everything was no problem and which allegedly cooperated with guardianship courts! I had to transfer 1600,00€ in advance to this detective agency, which I unfortunately did. I did not get any reasonable leads after that, nor what we discussed, simply nothing. But for this I had 1600,00€ in the sand, because I put so much hope in the support of this detective agency. That was the first and the last time I wanted to hire a detective agency to look for my daughter. Besides, all the money I had saved had gone for that. I would not have been able to afford a detective agency anymore. That was an involuntary lesson for me. My search had to go on! My search should go forward, but the lousy fraud of the detective agency, which I trusted and lost 1600,00€ for it, was heavy in my stomach! Next I had to check even more intensively whether a detective agency is authorized at all to search for a person in an incognito adoption. I asked around and investigated further,

 because I needed not only the support of the youth welfare offices, but I wanted to have my search further under own control. I trusted after my negative experiences no youth welfare office coworker, even if he/she still so endeavored to support a mother of origin, who looks for decades for their child. I tried to trust, but that was a long way and has also only been improved by the reliability of the Jugendamt employee from West Germany! Unfortunately, however, she could give me only conditional information, in order not to violate § 1758! It took me everything too long, constantly waiting for what I wished for decades?! I wanted to do something myself, as I had done the years before, because my own research brought me a bit closer to my goal of finding my daughter after every research that turned out positive. The proportion of youth welfare office employees contacted so far, on the other hand, was rather tiny! The information, or teachings about the personal status law and §1758, have taken a lot of time and it would never have led to my goal. So, itself is the woman and mother of origin, let's tackle it! Then again an idea came to me, of which I had heard and also read several times. I contacted an official tracing service! I wrote the application form and then patiently waited for the answer! I hoped for not too many questions. I not too many questions. I gave the search service the searched name - date of birth and address and that was it! Then came the big wait and hope, because even a tracing service can not do magic! It took 14 long days until I had mail in the mailbox from the tracing service. Finally I thought and the excitement rose with redness in my face. I was hot and I did not dare to open this longed-for letter from the tracing service. I put the letter on the living room table and stared at it for minutes. What might be written there?! Is it positive or negative? I looked as if spellbound at this letter! No matter, I thought either, or and I opened the letter. No, or, this is not true. I couldn't believe what was written there on the paper, from an authority. The person I was looking for was clearly identified! Enclosed was another letter from the commissioned tracing service, which again confirmed the date of birth of the wanted person. There was no more doubt! Name - address and the date of birth 16.09.1973 were clearly identified to this person. Since my confidence was in the cellar, I remained skeptical as always. Should it be so simple, I could not imagine that at all. But it would have been a dream, if it had been so simple! I had all the facts on the table, and yet I had to immediately reassure myself by phone with the tracing service and the responsible authority. It was the person I was looking for with name - date of birth and address! 100% clearly

 identified. All data were correctly evaluated by the authority and there was no error. Also the search service confirmed to me several times that there are no doubts in the official result and they have also explained to me exactly why these doubts are narrowed down by the authority from the beginning of the search. For example, there are 3 people with the same first or last name! It can also be that there are persons with the same name and address in the register. Therefore it is very important to specify the date of birth of the searched person in order to avoid error messages. If all 3 characteristics match - name - date of birth and address, then the searched person is clearly identified. If, on the other hand, only 2 characteristics match, e.g. name and address and the date of birth does not, then the person sought is not clearly identified and it is then also written on the official certificate. With my searched person all 3 characteristics agreed and therefore the person was clearly identified. Wonderful! This was the best news I got from this tracing service after decades of searching. I must admit that I did not know this either until I was confronted with it within my search. I was so very happy that I had contacted this reliable search service! But things were to turn out differently when I thought! After the search of the tracing service was successful, the wanted person was contacted.

 I wrote a personal letter and explained in it why I had called in a tracing service, in the great hope that this positive result would also make her happy. The employee of the tracing service pointed out to me that it could take a very long time until the person I was looking for would get back to me. Sometimes the wanted person never gets in touch at all, because he or she doesn't want to be contacted, or still needs time until the first contact is made. We now had to wait in peace! It passed 1 week - 2 weeks - 3 weeks and then I had a thick letter from the search service in my mailbox. Full of anticipation and good cheer I opened this longed-for letter from the tracing service. I could not believe my eyes! It was a nasty letter from the wanted person, from a lawyer. He threatened me with an injunction, if I do not leave the searched person immediately in peace, or let investigate over 3 persons. There rang nevertheless times again § 1758, which comes only with an incognito - adoption to the carrying, with me on. So, that was it then probably! With it she signaled to me completely clearly that she does not wish any contact to me. I did not understand the world any more, because I was looking for my daughter and wanted to get to know my daughter with all my heart. Now I was treated by strangers, like a criminal, that went decidedly too far. I was angry - disappointed and unspeakably sad. For me, it was like shooting at a sparrow with a cannon, because I did not mean did not want to harm anyone, except to look for and find my daughter. For me a world collapsed at that moment, why? I immediately called the Tracing Service and asked if they also got such a nasty letter from the lawyer, the wanted?! The employee of the Tracing Service said that such a thing can also happen, but rather very rarely. The largest part of the missing persons is pleased about contacts! She confirmed to me then also that they received also a letter from the lawyer and a prohibition further in the direction of the looked for person to investigate - Ausforschungsverbot also opposite 3 persons after § 1758, with incognito - adoptions! She choked me now also on the phone and said! We can help them unfortunately no more. Fortunately, they had helped me and the lawyer was relatively indifferent to me. He acted according to § 1758 and that is his duty, if an adopted person, no contact with his family of origin would like to have. I must honestly say that I was so disappointed that I did not want the person I was looking for to have my daughter's date of birth. Why didn't she talk to me? I don't think it's right to use such guns against a mother who only wants to know her child. But the trouble was to come to a head! Not only that a stranger lawyer with a

Injunction threatened and my search service thus eliminated, no it went even more blatantly against me and the search for my daughter. The father of my children never contacted me by phone! I could hardly get a word in edgewise as he was yelling nonstop in my ear. I would have claimed that his family adopted our daughter. I never claimed that and with that sentence and many other rash sentences, they single-handedly turned the focus of my search on themselves. Besides, I already knew it from stories of my former mother-in-law and my mother, where my daughter was probably adopted incognito. But it was going to get sharper! It was not enough for the clean family from West Germany to call in a lawyer against the search for my daughter, no then the father of the children should talk to me in my conscience with loud voice and impudent insults to my person. I asked myself, why is such a fuss made about a woman in the family from West Germany, when I am only looking for my daughter and why am I threatened with an injunction, when it is not my daughter that is being looked for! Question marks upon question marks paved my way. If it is not my daughter then why is everyone from West Germany/family of the biological father verbally attacking me. It was not over yet, because the family from West Germany called me even still impudently personally. What I there, from a

I was very surprised when I heard the words of the person I knew. With trembling voice she affirmed again and again that it is her daughter and that she has got her! Then I clarified her in the conversation what I have already for years for information about it and that I would never say that the woman would be my daughter. I was looking for my daughter and the road led me to her too! The other end of the phone went very quiet! I waited and hoped for the truth! This silence on the other end of the phone was eerie to me. I thought, what is going on and why is the relative from West Germany thinking so very long? Then I noticed how she thought about it, then said to me uncertainly and snappishly: And just like that my aunt told you that your daughter came to us after birth and we adopted her?! I said in a confident voice - Yes! She was silent for a moment and then tried to communicate with me. I did not understand the world anymore? We are all adults and what has happened, no one could undo and therefore I also presupposed that we could talk honestly with each other. No matter what the circumstances are, or were. I wanted to know exactly if it was her biological daughter and asked her in a friendly way if she could please send me the birth certificate of her daughter, or also send it to me through a lawyer, then the problem would be out of the world and I would be able to find her we could all sleep peacefully again! I assumed that if it is her biological daughter, it was also

 no problem to show me her birth certificate. On a birth certificate are the biological parents, where the child is born and e.g. in which birth clinic! If a child was adopted no birth certificate exists, but only a family record book entry, with the adoptive parents. Of course, for the sake of the child? These documents have nothing to do with reality and the adopted child grows up with a life lie! Whether this is really for the good of an adopted child, I find extremely questionable?! I believe that the adoptive parents are too afraid to tell their child that it is their child only before the adoption law, but that it has a family of origin and a mother who gave birth to her, or him. This would be fair to all the parents of origin, without these mothers you would not have these wonderful children by your side and could not call them your children! Families of origin deserve the greatest respect from the adoptive parents and not that you treat their parents of origin as enemies. Adopted children have 2 families! Their family of origin and their adoptive family. Respect and accept each other and pull together for the sake of your child. Then there is no need for blocking notes that make life hell for the birth parents. Let them participate in the life of their born children and don't limit them for always out of the life of your adopted children, because you love them both! This adoption path would be for all involved, the most humane solution and for the benefit of the adopted child. As they say, blood is thicker than water and family remains family! If people would work together and not constantly out of envy and jealousy against each other, then the adoption laws would be somewhat easier for the parents of origin and for the benefit of the adopted children! Envy and jealousy, is not a good advisor! Heart and love, is for the good of the adopted child! If you love your adopted child with all your heart, then you also accept his or her family of origin, who also love and miss their family member very much. No matter what circumstances have led to adoption. Every family of origin loves their child and family member and this contact should, if it is desired, be promoted and supported by the adoptive family - offices and authorities, instead of being ignored and pushed aside as I had to get to know it. On my numerous e-mails to offices and authorities I have met only blocking notes and refusals, as support, which would have really helped me to get to know my beloved daughter, sadly! I wanted to mention here again that the relative from West Germany did not send me a birth certificate of her daughter, not even through a lawyer! I can only say to this! If I had been in the same situation that someone thinks,

I adopted his child, then I would immediately help without thinking about it and show the birth certificate of my biological child. Where was there, the problem, if you have nothing to hide, or know something in secret! It was clear to me after this conversation that I could not expect any help from this family. People who only think about themselves and their advantages in life are not interested in parents of origin! Fortunately I had facts and that I had to owe only to my years of own researches! I was satisfied with myself and that I had come so far on my way of the search for my daughter. For me it was rather fate, if I met humans, who gave me without if and but, an answer to my questions and to those I am today very grateful. I think many people I met while searching for my daughter felt how desperate I was and supported me! Why did they support me? Because I was up to no evil, I just wanted to meet my child who was involuntarily given up for adoption, to tell her that I/we never forgot her on any day and on 9/16 of every year on her birthday, lit a candle just for her! That has been my goal for decades, to seek out my child to tell her that and to tell her the circumstances that led to her adoption! That was and is my goal! If there were not the countless incognito – adoption.

Blocking notes after § 1758 would be, which would put always and constantly boulders in my way with my search. By actions, like lawyers switch on after § 1758 Ausforschungsverbot, also over 3 persons, my search should be switched off, but where lay my offense?! I searched for my daughter, who was torn away from me with 15 years involuntarily by the youth welfare department in Berlin Neukölln and the family of the bodily father immediately after the birth and seen for me, to West Germany to her relatives was carried off. She is my daughter! I would not have given any of my children into foreign care. Even if I was only 15 years with the birth, on 16.09.1973, I was responsible enough and my family wanted to support me. This decision was made in favor of the biological father by his family and he never fought for his little daughter, until today! He prefers to put himself on the other side and pointed his finger threateningly at me?! They took away our daughter from us. How can you live with such guilt?! I gave birth to her and everyone left me alone in those difficult hours, but I got up and kept searching! My mother's heart led me on, to my goal! Love is stronger than your blocking adoption laws and § 1758. And nevertheless I must admit that these laws are strength-robbing and extremely annoying! They want to bring the parents of origin to their knees, the search for to give up their adopted children! If everyone who is looking for his/her child

 is aware of this, then he/she does not waste his/her energy on these laws, but focuses his/her positive energies into the search. It was not a walk in the park to this day to search for my daughter, but my prescription was not to give up, for my daughter who should not live with a life lie. Because every person on this earth has a right to know his origin and his roots. So slowly it had made the rounds, also with the central adoption offices, which I had received due to my search, a bad letter after § 1758 Ausforschungsverbot also opposite 3 persons, like search services and other authorities, from the lawyer of the woman contacted by the search service. My thoughts were on this! If she has nothing to do with it, why this family makes itself so many trouble, in order to keep me away! I did not believe in coincidence in this case. Much does not help much, but makes suspicious! I especially remembered the sentence in the letter from this lawyer. There it is written! Even if it is not about your wanted daughter, we would like to ask you not to contact the family from West Germany any more, because they bring unrest into your life?! Question: How can I bring unrest into a life if there is no connection? Made-up nonsense to make § 1758 look good. Why does the family at all against me a lawyer, if yes there is nothing that has to do with my search,

 funny coincidence, isn't it? Honestly? How stupid do you think I am! I am not 15 years more, but a grown woman who is a family and social therapist by profession since 1991! But even if I didn't have a social profession, I would look for my daughter because, like every mother of origin, I have a mother's heart and that is what leads all of us who look for their children to the goal. Heart and mind, are the most important in the search for his adopted child to reach the goal! If I hadn't finished my research before the friendly lawyer letter, I'm sure it would have been a bit more complicated, but that was the point in it! Come time, come advice! I was satisfied with my research and that was all that mattered to me! The others didn't ask about me either, or support me in my search. I was a lone fighter with random information that no one really wanted to give me. The way is the goal! But I am also only a human being and wanted to take a break for a few months and collect myself after these negative experiences, to think about whether my search is now finished, or whether there would still be something to do! Anyway, I needed rest and time for other things! Please, the sentence, I needed time for other things in life do not understand wrong, but this decades-long search for my beloved daughter, is also strength-sapping. Especially when these negative things, like nasty letters from lawyers on the other side

Lawyers of the opposite side threaten to slay a person with their § 1758. then one needs first of all rest, in order to activate the strength, to look further and not to give up. Unfortunately, that's not always so easy when there are constant obstacles put in your way by everyone involved! After a few months, I had regained my strength and thought about what my next step would be. But I also thought about § 1758, which had to be observed. I was just immersed in my thoughts when my phone rang and who was on the line? The Central Adoption Office from West Germany! I was a bit taciturn and wanted to wait first what the friendly employee had to announce to me. She asked me whether I had also received a letter from a lawyer of Mrs. C. a few months ago? Without much ado I fetched the letter from the lawyer and read it to the employee from the Central Adoption Office from West Germany. She listened, as so often before, only devoutly to my words. Then she said to me, I would now like to comment on this, because I had received a call from Mrs. C.. I had a very long conversation with Mrs. C. and I should tell them that what was done to them as a 15-year-old girl is quite terrible and she is very sorry. It was also never talked about in her family. If it is so then she would have lived with a life lie over decades and that would be very hard to

 and she needs her rest now! So it was noted then in the file by the central adoption office from West Germany. I had to take note of that and that was the end of the conversation with the employee of the Central Adoption Office for the time being. I thanked for the information and was also disappointed, over this reaction, on my decades-long search, for my child! I searched for the meaning of my search, because that was neither a yes, nor a no, whether I found my daughter. I was told by a very wise woman during the course of my search. You will never find out exactly if it is your daughter or not, § 1758, but I will give you some good advice! Listen to your mother's heart, because it never lies to you! My mother's heart told me that I have found my daughter long ago! And that already years before my intensive search for her. Because I have received through fate so many clues that led to my daughter, that I was quite sure. But unfortunately feelings alone are not enough to prove that and that is why I collected written clues that led to my daughter for decades. A puzzle, where part by part was put together until a picture emerged. My picture was unfortunately not yet perfect, because here and there still puzzle pieces were missing. Some fit and some did not yet fit into my puzzle picture! So my search went on again, to track down further clues that led to my daughter. The employee of the Central

 Adoptionsstelle gave me the hint to contact the Zentrale Adoptionsstelle in Berlin again. Maybe they have already made some progress with their research on my daughter? This was rather a red rag for me, because I had contacted them years ago. I went there in person and the employee wanted to get in touch with me and that was years ago. How should I trust these coworkers of the central adoption place from Berlin, if they do not hold themselves to agreements with parents of origin and not even for necessary to give notice whether the search was successful, or not. If with an incognito adoption the § 1758 will always stand in between, one can deal honestly with the parents of origin and not make them false hopes that he/she would get information. I was already, through my decades of searching for my child annoyed by the § 1758. I needed time to think about whether I wanted this. What did this employee from West Germany know about where I had asked for help everywhere to assist me in my search. I had begged and asked politely enough at the offices and agencies, but they kept talking their way out of it, or sending other employees to their agency phone when I asked uncomfortable questions. At some point one

As a mother of origin, I no longer feel like saying thank you for any information. Isn't that understandable, dear

 parents of origin? Also as a mother of origin/family one cannot bend only before the offices and authorities and beg constantly for the fact that one gets support. Why is this support only offered to adoptees? As a family of origin one does not dare at all to contact the central adoption offices, because there already on their Internet sides friendly one refers to the fact that they support Adoptierte those their families of origin search, gladly and also gladly try, if the Adoptierte it wishes to contact the family of origin and the contact, if this should come off, gladly to accompany and psychologically support. For the families of origin remains either no room, or only very few possibilities to be supported! Of course also families of origin get support, from the central adoption offices? Let's put it this way! I call the Central Adoption Office, as a mother of origin and tell the staff that I have been looking for my daughter for decades and need their support, because I am not allowed to look into the files. Adoptees are allowed to look at adoption files if they want to know their family of origin. A family of origin is not allowed to see anything at all, except to wait for a case-by-case decision from the gracious staff member to hope who will take care of this story. Maybe he/she then decides to support the family of origin in their

 search?! This could take years, as was the case with me. Why? Incognito - adoption, according to § 1758. The incognito - adoption is the worst form of adoption! Unfortunately, I was not allowed to be choosy! Even if I researched for decades alone after my child, I needed the support of the central adoption offices and that were for me 2 contacts. I came in my years of search again and again to limits where I could not go further without coming into conflict with § 1758. Detectives and search services, I could also use only limited to support my search. And after the lawyer had threatened me with § 1758, the doors were closed. With all love to my daughter, but I have been guilty of nothing all my life and did not want to be reported innocently, because of § 1758. I wanted to go the legal way, to look for my daughter and hopefully find her that way! That was my largest hope, because my mother heart had to suffer unspeakably since the birth of my children to 16.09.1973 in Berlin - Neukölln. I thought again about it, what the friendly woman employee, the central adoption place in West Germany had advised me. She was also so kind and sent me all important contact data of the Central Adoption Office in Berlin. I still resisted inwardly against it, the

Central Adoption Office on Berlin, because I had personally contacted them a few years ago and no one cared about my search or about contacting my daughter. It was simply no longer contacted and my request to search for my daughter officially ignored. Unfortunately, I had to cope with this again and again! Even if the adoption laws and with an incognito - adoption § 1758 stands in between, the coworkers should remain honest and not make false hopes for an origin mother/family over years to be allowed to become acquainted with the loved child by an establishment of contact over the central adoption offices. I had never made any claims to my daughter because I gave birth to her, but my mother's heart only wanted to get to know her child, which was cruelly snatched away from me after its birth, by the Youth Welfare Office in Berlin - Neukölln. On the next day it was then so far! I had decided to contact the Central Adoption Office in Berlin, even though I did not expect anything from it. But times have changed and now I had not only the reason to find my daughter, but another reason, which is anchored in the Basic Law. I was curious to see the reaction of the staff at the Central Adoption Office when I confronted them with the basic law of adoption laws. However, I was not sure if they already knew about it, because the Central

Adoption Office on West Germany I had already informed about my new findings. I still considered, whether I put the inquiry with the central adoption office in Berlin in writing by E-Mail, or whether I contacted them rather personally by telephone?! I decided for a personal call! The first employee, from her I had received the contact data, from the Central Adoption Office in West Germany, could not be reached by telephone. I did not want to be satisfied with that, because there was official office hours there that day and I had also called there during that time. I looked for another coworker out of the contact list over Internet, from the central adoption place in Berlin out and I had luck! There a very friendly woman employee came to the telephone! I introduced myself and asked cautiously whether the employee of the Central Adoption Agency from West Germany is known to her? As an answer she gave me a YES. Then I could talk freely and she listened attentively. Then I told her about the human genetic examination in the family and that it is written in the Basic Law of Adoption that an adopted child must know about it because it is his/her roots! Then also § 1758 steps with an incognito - adoption out of force, because it concerns the origin of the adopted child. That would be then also again individual case decisions, the central adoption offices. I believe, if the reasoning would not have been so important that my daughter must learn urgently of it, then I would have considered again to contact the central adoption office of Berlin to the 2 times. But in this case it was my duty, opposite my daughter, because whether adopted, or not, she has our origin roots! The Central Adoption Offices saw this immediately and offered to support me so that my daughter would know about it! Then I had to send some important documents to the Central Adoption Office in Berlin by mail. Then I had to show a lot of patience again, but I was used to waiting for decades. After 10 days of waiting I started to get restless, because I asked myself what was taking so long to get some information? I sat down at my PC and wrote the friendly employee of the Central Adoption Office in Berlin a message in which I asked if she could tell me something about my request. In relatively short time, a friendly, but very short e-mail came back from this coworker, with the words - unfortunately I can write them still no new message! I will get back to them when I have heard back. I thought, that's a great reply to me, without any information where it was asked or why it was asked? That was no answer for me! Now I had to wait endless days and weeks again! Nothing happened and I suspected nothing good! After 14 days I called the employee, of the Central Adoption Office in Berlin and hoped that she would answer her phone. No response to my call! The disappointment and the distrust towards the authority rose high in me and I remembered the years before, where the employee of this central adoption office left me literally in the rain with my requests to her to support me in the search for my daughter and never contacted me again! That was it again, I thought! 10 minutes later on the same day I tried again with a phone call to the employee and lo and behold a miracle happened, but it was not this employee! It was another friendly colleague in her place at her phone number. I didn't believe it, what are they up to, I asked myself! The colleague is no longer in the house today, said the colleague of the employee who was responsible for my request. I thanked her and could have cried, wondering what is going on now again that I apparently no longer get any information. I did not want to put up with this procedure again, because my concern is in the basic law of the adoption laws and I will refer to that. My daughter must learn from my important request! I did not let go and called the next day immediately again with the central adoption place in Berlin, under the same telephone number, in order to reach the woman employee, who was responsible for my request. I was relieved, because the employee was on the phone! I noticed immediately that her behavior towards me had changed completely since she had commissioned investigations to find my daughter. before that we could talk freely and unconstrained, nevertheless she told me from the beginning of our conversations that if she should meet my daughter during her investigations and it was about an incognito - adoption, she unfortunately may not give me any information about it! There he was again! Like a warning sign it stood before my mental eye § 1758. She would have to speak first with her leader, what she may tell me and what not. Now it was that time again! She had learned something about the adoption of my daughter and was not allowed to talk about it! I wondered how it should go on now and especially how my daughter should find out about it. I was as 1000 times before helpless and I felt again left alone by the authorities. I did not know any more, what I should say to this for me negative message and said goodbye for the time being to the coworker, the central adoption place in Berlin, which was silent only the remainder of our discussion! in the meantime I received an email from the central adoption place from West Germany, with no better news! all were now together endeavored to work on my request for me and my daughter, but I should not experience of it any more. I did not want to stand like that and sat down at my PC! I researched about incognito adoption laws and the § 1758 and by chance, or also fate I saw in the Internet an information about the adoption laws. Since I was not really interested in these adoption laws, I have mostly seen them for years, just skimmed over them. Now however I made myself the trouble to read these adoption laws and the § 1758 with incognito - adoption attentively, in the hope to find a door, where my daughter must be contacted also by the youth welfare department, because of her origin roots! I had great hope to find the famous needle in the haystack and so it was fortunately then also. Here it was written, the basic law of the adoption law! That was my ticket, around that, that youth welfare department had to become active, whether it wanted there, or not! because law is law and the basic law for adopted persons, is anchored there! That may not be ignored by the youth welfare offices. Unfortunately they wanted to ignore my important request again! I did not want to be suppressed and continued to fight for my daughter and my concern to the staff of the Central Adoption Office in Berlin. I sent the employee of the youth welfare department this information in written law form and waited, what would come back there?! Or is my request further ignored? Ignored not really, but it was again only tacitly from the Mitarbeiterin to the knowledge taken! I received of course for the time being no further message! My last state of the conversation was, that she may give me no more information, if it concerns my adopted daughter. What should I still do? All efforts were in vain and the offices remained stubborn, no matter which adoption laws I presented to them. I felt really stupid and made fun of by the youth welfare offices. I was literally fed up with the Central Adoption Offices - authorities and offices and I needed a break. I resolved not to contact them anymore, no matter where! I was fed up with having to beg for support from the youth welfare offices all the time. They don't even take health matters seriously, which my daughter has to learn from the basic law, and I don't feel like constantly running after their information, only to be turned away or put off. I knew who my daughter is and only that counted for me! They don't need to tell me anything else for all I care, I thought, opening my email inbox. Is this true or am I dreaming? The Youth Welfare Office! I had received an e-mail from the head of the Central Adoption Office in Berlin and I was very surprised! The e-mail was kindly written and she received information for me, as the mother of origin. This information received no clues to my search, for my child! It was held as always to § 1758 from official side. I can only say, it was a friendly e-mail, but it contained unfortunately no information about my concerns! The first joy, replaced the disappointment and I stood as always alone there, with my search. In this e-mail I, as a mother of origin received conditions, which I wanted to question again. I wrote a friendly e-mail to the employee back and asked why they have to fulfill these conditions and whether they would have taken up contact with my daughter, or? I sent this e-mail and then was again the big wait announced. Nothing happened for days! I got on my important questions, simply no answers, as so often before. It annoyed me, because it was always the same procedure. Demands were made on me by the youth welfare offices, but if I had a question and wanted information about it, I got no real answer. Or beautifully paraphrased words on paper, according to § 1758. Why did I never get rid of the feeling that I was given answers, but what it was really about, the contact with my daughter, was beautifully framed omitted and that made me sad and tired. Not one of the staff spoke a frank word to me! Sad, but true! My own research has taken me a long way over decades. It all started in 1973 with my mother's passport, which was to be shredded in the women's clinic in Berlin. Thank you, because I could build on it, which was certainly not planned by you. Because you have my children death silent and symbolically buried! My mother's heart knew that my daughter had survived. What you wanted to prevent, shame on all of you who were involved in this rotten intrigue! You made a whole family unhappy and took away a baby that would have had a future with his family. You let my child grow up with a life lie?! How does that make you feel? Do you have any human feelings at all? Or are you all just pure selfishness towards a family of origin who miss their family members. I feel so violated and deported because I am their mother who gave birth to them not just for all of you. I deserve respect and not lies! As always, I waited for an e-mail from the employee of the Berlin Youth Welfare Office. Actually, I had long ago resolved to ask there no more, because I get anyway no information as a mother of origin. On the other hand, I was interested in what the next answer would be. I asked by E-Mail again politely, how the coworkers decided, to my important request?! The next day an e-mail came, which was rather short. Nothing would be decided yet and I must be patient until the next week. I told myself that it was useless to get angry. I was already happy about the fact that there was an answer in my e-mail and now, as always, patience was the order of the day. Since you need nerves of steel and yet after so many decades, without any further support from the authorities, I was really exhausted and therefore I had to take more and more breaks. I knew exactly when I should stop contacting some authorities. Exactly then, when I noticed that the information doors were closed more and more by the employees. That was the time when I received less and less to no answers to my requests! Sometimes I would then try to follow up by phone. Then the colleague was out of the office, coincidentally had vacation, was on advanced training, or simply not at her place! No one knew when she would be back at her desk. If I had then nevertheless times luck, which was this woman coworker even on the telephone, I received a friendly, but determining, we may give them no more information over the adoption of their daughter! Then I knew, here the office door is closed. I had no other choice but to hope for the favor of the employees of the youth welfare offices, which became more and more difficult. To me, my search seemed endless and the reactions from the responsible staff did not make my concerns about never being allowed to meet my daughter in my life any better. They took away my hope some days, weeks and months! Those were the times I wanted to quit. This endless search, for the needle in the haystack!

I wanted to keep fighting and never would I have given up.

Closing words

Who fights can lose!
Who stops fighting has lost!
I have decided to fight until the last day to establish contact with my daughter!
Wishes unfortunately do not come true 100%, but I am very satisfied and happy with my positive result after decades of searching! Because I have convinced to be a mother of origin who loves her daughter above everything and I have not let myself be turned away by any authority because of § 1758. I and my little daughter have become victims of wrong decisions and foreign regulations in the year 1973, of offices and authorities. My only offense was that I was only 15 years old and underage at your birth! My child I love you with all my heart and I will always love you, because you will always be a part of me. The positive result, what I wanted to achieve, I have achieved! For support I was offered an accompanied sibling contact, if it is desired by all! That was my goal, for my son, because he was also cheated of his biological sister for decades. I have a hope again and that feels good. Parents of origin never forget and never give up looking for your children. Because they are a part of you, good luck! Thank you so much, to everyone who supported me!
A mother's heart never forgets and my search is over in 2019!

Dedication for my twin daughters.

Both girls were born on 16.09.1973 on Berlin.
My daughter Thea died on 18.09.1973 in the children's hospital in Berlin - Neukölln.
I love you my child and could not be with you.
To hold you in my arms To say goodbye to you forever. That you died two days after your birth? I only found out in 2023. Through further research and evidence. It was a rocky road to find you. To finally be able to make peace. What did they do to me, you and your sister? There are neither words of comfort for it! Nor apologies. And yet we must make peace with it together. We cannot bring back the past. I have never regretted a day that I searched for you and found you. I love you! Your mom.

Acknowledgement

I would like to express my sincere thanks to all the people. Who accompanied me on my long and hard way of searching for my twin daughters, comforted me and opened doors for me. Only together we are strong. Thank you!

To my loyal readers!

I thank you all that you have fought with me the time of my search at my side. To search for my daughters. I never gave up and found them both. Even though my search lasted over 40 years. I have never regretted a day. Because I have even if my path was rocky. I reached my goal. If you have not yet found your children. I wish you much strength and do not give up. Because who gives up will lose. I have never given up! Thank you! Your Brigitte Kohrs